# Machine well off:
# how anybody can procure six figures from home with a straightforward Accounting business

By
## JOANNA MIDDLETON

**Disclaimer**

The information in this book is intended for general knowledge purposes only and should not be considered a substitute for professional advice. The author makes no representation or warranty as to the accuracy or completeness of the information. The author assumes no liability for any damages resulting from the use of this information.

# Table of contents

# Introduction

The sum that you can procure as a passage-level clerk will differ as it does inside most jobs, contingent upon things like insight.

As per research, the typical rate is $21 each hour for individuals who function as a clerk full-time.

If you are maintaining your own accounting business, you can charge any costs you need! You can likewise take on various clients and procure more that way too.

This book will teach you step-by-step instructions on how to make that money from home.

# Chapter 1: Beginning

Bookkeeping is the most well-known approach to recording your association's money-related trades into composed accounts reliably. It can similarly imply the different recording strategies associations can use. Bookkeeping is an essential piece of your accounting communication for several reasons. At the point when you keep exchange records refreshed, you can create precise monetary reports that assist with estimating business execution. Nitty gritty records will likewise be convenient in case of a duty review.

# Techniques for accounting

Before you start accounting, your business should conclude what technique you will follow. While picking, consider the volume of day-to-day exchanges your business has and how much income you procure. On the off chance that you are an independent venture, a perplexing accounting strategy intended for endeavors might cause superfluous complexities. On the other hand, less powerful strategies for accounting won't do the trick for huge enterprises.

Given this, we should separate these strategies so you can track down the right one for your business.

## Single-passage accounting

Single-passage accounting is a direct technique where one section is made for every exchange in your books. These exchanges are normally kept up within a money book to follow approaching income and active costs. You don't require formal bookkeeping to prepare for the single-passage framework. The single-section technique will suit little privately owned businesses and sole ownerships that don't trade using a loan, own practically no actual resources, and hold modest quantities of stock.

## Twofold passage accounting

Twofold passage accounting is more vigorous. It follows the rule that each exchange influences something like two records, and they are recorded as charges and credits. For instance, on the off chance that you make a deal for $10, your money record will be charged for $10 and your business record will be credited by a similar sum. In the twofold passage framework, the all-out credits should constantly approach the all-out charges. At the point when this occurs, your books are "adjusted."

Involving the twofold passage technique for accounting appears to be legit assuming your business is huge, public, or trades using a loan. Undertakings frequently pick the twofold passage framework since it leaves less leeway. As it were, it 'twofold checks' your books because every exchange is recorded as two coordinating but balancing accounts.

## Cash-based or gathering-based

The subsequent stage is picking either money or gathering reasons for your accounting. This choice will rely upon how your business perceives its income and costs.

In real money-based, you perceive income when you get cash into your business. Costs are perceived when they are paid for. At the end of the day, any time cash enters or leaves your records, they are perceived in the books. This implies that buys or deals made on layaway won't go into your books until the money trades.

In the accumulation technique, income is perceived when it is acquired. Likewise, costs are recorded when they are brought about, generally alongside related incomes. The genuine money doesn't need to enter or exit for the exchange to be recorded. You can stamp your deals and buys made using a credit card immediately.

Both a money and gathering premise can work with single- or twofold passage accounting. Overall nonetheless, the single-passage strategy is the establishment of cash-based accounting. Exchanges are recorded as single passages which are either cash coming in or going out. The gathering premise works better with the twofold passage framework.

# The most effective method to keep sections in accounting

Creating fiscal summaries like asset reports, pay proclamations, and income explanations assists you with understanding where your business stands and measuring its exhibition. For these reports to depict your business precisely, you should have appropriately archived records of your exchanges. Keeping these records however current as conceivable seems to be additionally useful while accommodating your records.

Recording exchanges start with source archives like buy and deal orders, bills, solicitations, and sales register tapes. When you accumulate these archives, you can record the exchanges utilizing diaries, records, and the preliminary equilibrium. If you are a tiny organization, you may just need a sales register. The data can then be merged and transformed into fiscal summaries.

Sales registers

A sales register is an electronic machine that is utilized to work out and enlist exchanges. Typically, sales registers are utilized to keep income in stores. The clerk gathers the money for a deal and returns an equilibrium added up to the client. Both the gathered money and equilibrium returned are kept in the register as single-passage cash accounts. Sales enlists also store exchange receipts, so you can without much of a stretch record them in your deals diary.

Sales registers are usually tracked down in organizations, everything being equal. Notwithstanding, they aren't typically the essential strategy for recording exchanges since they utilize the single-section, cash-based process for accounting. This makes them helpful for tiny organizations however excessively oversimplified for ventures.

<u>The diary</u>

The diary is known as the book of unique passages. It is where a business sequentially records its exchanges interestingly. A diary can be either physical (as a book or journal), or computerized (put away as calculation sheets, or information in bookkeeping programming). It indicates the date of every exchange, the records credited or charged, and the sum in question. While the diary isn't generally checked for balance toward the finish of the monetary year, every diary section influences the record. As we'll learn, it is basic that the record is adjusted, so keeping an exact diary is a positive routine to keep. This structure is valuable for twofold section accounting.

## The record

A record is a book or a gathering of records. It is likewise called the book of second passages. After you enter exchanges in a diary, they are characterized into isolated records and afterward moved into the record. These records are translated by accounts in the request: resources, liabilities, value, pay, and costs. Like the diary, the record can likewise be physical or electronic bookkeeping sheets.

A record contains an outline of records, which is a rundown of the relative multitude of names and number of records in the record. The graph generally happens in a similar request of records as the translated records.

Not at all like the diary, records are examined by reviewers, so they should constantly be adjusted toward the finish of the financial year. If the complete charges are more than the all-out credits, it's known as a charge balance. On the off chance that the all-out credits offset the complete charges, there is a credit balance. The record is significant in twofold passage accounting where every exchange changes no less than two sub-record accounts.

<u>Preliminary equilibrium</u>
The preliminary equilibrium is delivered from the accumulated and summed-up record passages. The preliminary equilibrium resembles a test to check whether your books are adjusted. It records the records precisely in the accompanying request: resources, liabilities, value, pay, and costs with the consummation account balance.

A bookkeeper as a rule creates the preliminary equilibrium to see where your business stands and how well your books are adjusted. This can then be cross-checked against records and diaries. The awkward nature of charges and attributes is not difficult to recognize in the preliminary equilibrium. However, it isn't generally mistake-free. Any misinterpreted or wrongly-translated diary passage in the record can cause an erroneous preliminary equilibrium. It is ideal to pay special attention to blunders early and write them on the record as opposed to hanging tight for the preliminary equilibrium toward the finish of the monetary year.

## Fiscal summaries

The following, and presumably the main, move toward accounting is to create fiscal summaries. These assertions are ready by uniting data from the passages you have recorded on an everyday premise. They give an understanding of your organization's presentation after some time, uncovering the regions you want to enhance. The three significant monetary reports that each business should be aware of and comprehend are the income proclamation, accounting report, and pay explanation.

## The income articulation

The income explanation is precisely the exact thing its name recommends. A monetary report tracks approaching and active money in your business. It permits you (and financial backers) to comprehend how well your organization handles obligations and costs. By summing up this information, you can check whether you are making sufficient money to run a supportable, beneficial business.

## The monetary record

The monetary record reports a business's resources, liabilities, and investor's value at a given moment. In basic words, it lets you know what your business claims, lowes, and the sum contributed by investors. In any case, the monetary record is just a preview of a business's monetary situation for a specific date. It should be contrasted with accounting reports of different periods also. The monetary record permits you to comprehend the liquidity and monetary design of your business through examinations like current proportion, resource turnover proportion, stock turnover proportion, and obligation-to-value proportion.

## The pay articulation

The pay proclamation, likewise called the benefit and misfortune explanation, centers around the income acquired and expenses caused by a business after some time. There are two sections in a run-of-the-mill pay explanation. The upper half records working pay while the lower half records consumptions. The assertion tracks these over a period, like the last quarter of the monetary year. It shows how the net income of your business is changed over into net profit which results in one or the other benefit or shortfall. The pay articulation doesn't zero in on receipts or money subtleties.

## Bank compromise

Bank compromise is the most common way of finding coinciding between the exchanges in your ledger and the exchanges in your accounting records. Accommodating your financial balances is a basic move toward accounting because, after all the other things are logged, it is the last move toward tracking down errors in your books. Bank compromise helps you do nothing not right about your cash.

For what reason is it obligatory?
Bank compromise is a must because it:
- Gives what is going on in your organization
- Tracks income precisely
- Recognizes extortion or bank mistakes

## Transforming $0 into $100

Clerks work with monetary exchanges and monetary records before they get disregarded by a bookkeeper.

Clerks care for monetary information on all the more an everyday premise and utilize those fiscal summaries to make reports and calculation sheets.

They'll make monetary reports, update any monetary records, and tackle errands like paying solicitations, sending solicitations, dealing with creditor liabilities, and so forth.

The budget summaries and reports then are given to bookkeepers or evaluating agents to survey and perceive how they impact the business.
You can turn into a guaranteed clerk, however, it isn't needed, nor do you want a four-year college education in bookkeeping.

The amount Do Clerks Acquire?
The sum that you can procure as a passage-level clerk will differ as it does inside most jobs, contingent upon things like insight.

As per research, the typical rate is $21 each hour for individuals who function as a clerk full-time.

If you are maintaining your own accounting business, you can charge any costs you need! You can likewise take on various clients and procure more that way too.

**4 Stages For How To Turn into A Clerk**

1. Clerk Preparing

If you have any desire to turn into a clerk and begin a business, there are a couple of accounting abilities you'll have to survey and make budget reports and bookkeeping sheets:

- Critical thinking
- Variable-based math (math overall!)
- Association
- Scrupulousness (conscientious)

- Respectability/Classification

PC abilities (composing, utilizing some accounting programming, Success, and so forth.) Presently, you needn't bother with a Four-year certification to turn into a clerk, however, essentially a secondary school degree is suggested.

Numerous organizations might maintain that you should have instruction if you don't have insight since you'll be working with their monetary exchanges.

You can gain from accounting courses or show yourself accounting skills. You can show yourself accounting by doing precisely everything you're doing-investigating and perusing.

You can understand websites and books to turn into an effective clerk or even watch YouTube recordings to figure it out.

Watching recordings on the most proficient method to utilize QuickBooks and different projects will be truly useful in fostering your tech abilities as a bookkeeper.     Structure Your Business

When you become a clerk, all you want for your own virtual accounting business is a PC arrangement with the works and some accounting programming, such as QuickBooks.

Accounting positions require this kind of programming, and you'll have to get it to chip away at the books for your clients.

Then, you'll require a protected association, as you'll be working with secret and confidential information from your clients.

When you have the nuts and bolts at home, you can make your business ready!

2. You can make at least a couple sorts of organizations:
A sole ownership and a restricted responsibility organization (LLC) are the most well-known.

The sort you register as really depends on you and what your business needs are.

You'll need to make a site, perhaps utilizing WordPress, so clients can see what administrations you deal with and how you would help them as a clerk.

Promoting your business is vital, and it's the last step before you search for your most memorable accounting position and track down clients.

3. Go after Positions On the web and Gain Clients
Now that you've been prepared and have your business begun, now is the right time to get on the

accounting profession way by landing some accounting positions on the web.

You want to acquire clients or your business will not be around for a long time!

You ought to sort out the number of clients you need to have at a given time and how long you're willing to function.

Occupations you can have practical experience in for clients incorporate finance, monetary reports like pay proclamations or asset reports, charge readiness, or another particular help.

You ought to have a resume arranged and have it show the projects and bookkeeping programming you're fit for utilizing.
Remember to include any conventional schooling you have, particularly a Four-year college

education or confirmation they aren't needed, however, make you contrast the opposition.

The more you gain insight, the more clients you'll attract.

Track down Clients As A Consultant: You can pursue destinations like Fiverr and Flex Tasks to acquire occupations and track down clients.

4. Think about Turning into A Confirmed Clerk
You'll likewise need to think about turning into an ensured clerk, as you can get seriously prepared on the most proficient method to turn into a clerk yet in addition to that!

Accreditation will make you more interesting to clients, and you can charge something else for your administrations!

A confirmed clerk can charge upwards of $25+ each hour!

When you're a guaranteed public clerk, you might require proceeding with instructions to keep current on bookkeeping changes.

However, the projects you join will tell you what kind of proceeding the training you'll need and where to get extra assets.

What Are the Stars versus Cons of Turning into a Clerk?

Similarly, as with most positions, there are advantages and disadvantages, and it's eventually down to you to conclude what you are content with doing.

Masters

You get to set your rates

You can take on however many clients as you wish

It's an adaptable professional way, you pick your hours and work time

You want PC abilities, to have the option to utilize accounting sheets, to peruse monetary exchanges, and so forth.

You can do this as a side gig to fit in around work you have presently or your kids' timetables

You might require a secondary school degree, however, no different degrees are fundamental

Cons

- You should track down your clients and pitch to them
- Your pay may not be steady from one month to another toward the start

- You want to know a great deal you should be gifted in bookkeeping programming and steady in how well you make monetary reports
- Affirmed accountants truly do make all the more hourly, so you might need to go the additional step and put the turn-out in for accreditation

**Planning your fantasies by numbers**

1. Record What You Need to Accomplish: When your deepest desires stay in your mind, they turn out to be barely noticeable. To cause them to appear to be more "genuine," it assists with discussing them or recording them on paper. This can cause your fantasies to feel more substantial and permit you to thoroughly consider them in a more profound, more significant way.

2. Make a Dream Board: The vision board fills in as a visual sign of the positive things you need

to pursue in your life. When you make a dream leading to the objectives you need to accomplish — and how you need to feel when you accomplish them — you ought to keep it where you can see it consistently to assist you with remaining persuaded to continue onward.

3. Separate Every Objective Into More Modest Steps: There's nothing bad about needing to accomplish a major objective, however, you need to work in reverse from that point to recognize the more modest advances you can take that will get you to the end goal. Training stage BetterUp suggests making an 'objective stepping stool' by composing your principal objective at the top crosspiece of the stepping stool," then, at that point, adding things to do to each step on the stepping stool to be clear about "the more modest objectives you want to accomplish to accomplish your primary objective." The objective stepping stool is

simply a visual device you can use to outline an arrangement to vanquish your fantasies.

4. Remain Positive, Even With Setbacks: When you're hopeful about accomplishing your fantasies regardless of misfortunes you could insight, you're bound to achieve them in the long haul.

5. Gain From Disappointment and Change Accordingly: When you do encounter disappointment, you can utilize your positive outlook to transform the untimely obstacle into a positive growth opportunity. Encountering a misfortune or snag is not a sign that you ought to quit attempting to try the impossible; it's an opportunity for you to only change your strategies for how you will accomplish your objectives. Furthermore, when you at long last achieve your fantasy, it will be that much better.

# Chapter 2: Gaining Customers

Promoting is the most common way of bringing thought, item, or administration before a purchasing crowd. Showcasing centers around a client's needs and needs so organizations can recognize who could buy their item to draw in those clients to the business.

# The main thing clients are concerned about

We'll investigate the characteristics that make an optimal accounting client.

1. Association: The underpinning of good accounting is efficient monetary records. An ideal client keeps up with their archives, receipts, and monetary information in a methodical way. This not only facilitates the clerk's responsibility (and holds expenses down!) yet in addition guarantees precise and exceptional monetary records.
2. Idealness: Having opportune outcomes is a significant element of good monetary detailing. Clients who are immediately given monetary information and reports assist with keeping monetary records exact and current. This training forestalls the gathering of an excess of monetary data.
3. Correspondence: Viable openness is of the utmost importance for any effective

relationship, including the one between a client and their clerk. Clients who are open and responsive while examining monetary objectives, changes in their business, or resolving different kinds of feedback, add to a useful working relationship.

4. Trustworthiness and Straightforwardness: Ideal clients speak the truth about their monetary circumstances and are straightforward about any monetary issues or disparities. This straightforwardness guarantees that the monetary experts can give precise and applicable counsel to clients.

5. Responsiveness: Fast reactions to accountant inquiries or solicitations for extra data can forestall postponements and mistakes. A responsive client guarantees the accounting system moves along as expected.

6. Understanding: Understanding the significance of accounting and being willing to work intimately with your clerk to

accomplish monetary objectives is a fundamental nature of a decent client.

7. Consistency: Consistent clients comply with burden regulations and guidelines. This is significant for precise and lawful monetary detailing, and it's the obligation of both the client and the accountant.

8. Regarding Proficient Skill: Clients who trust their clerk and bookkeeper's mastery and counsel can make a positive and useful working relationship. Accounting subject matter experts and bookkeepers are prepared experts who can offer significant bits of knowledge.

9. Consistency: Consistency in monetary practices and information passage is crucial to keeping up with exact and dependable records. Routineness in giving information helps stay up with the latest.

10. Persistence: Accounting can include complex errands and clients who show

persistence and comprehension of the interaction add to a positive and compelling relationship.

An ideal accounting client is somebody who imparts well, esteems the assistance, is focused on keeping up with monetary exactness, and works cooperatively with their accounting group to accomplish their monetary objectives. By focusing on your monetary housekeeping, you can guarantee an effective clerk-client relationship!

## If you disdain to sell, do this all things being equal

1. Ditch pointless administrative work

Alright, so not all paper will go.

The paperless office resembles a sci-fi car capable of flying: consistently anticipated however never entirely showing up. In any case, it would be difficult to contend you want all that paper in your office when there's a product out there that can handle accounting all the more effectively. The paper issue is the army.

It gets lost or misfiled; espresso gets spilled on it; you use it to jot notes when a client calls and afterward coincidentally discard it; it's difficult to find reports when you want them, (for example, at charge documenting time); and staying up with the latest is troublesome.

What you can do
The more you record carefully, the speedier it is to get to and the less time you spend doing the books.

Use bookkeeping programming for your accounting (indeed, believe it or not, a decent bookkeeping arrangement will permit you to do the books and significantly more as well) to clean up your work area of all that paper.

## 2. Digitalise your receipts

Assuming you included constant spending assembling, arranging, and recording receipts, you'd lament not spending it on additional useful undertakings. The most concerning issue can be tracking down them. On the off chance that you maintain a business moving, they could be anyplace. When they stack up, they're hard to handle.

Getting on top of them removes an increasingly large piece from the day, so you put them off interminably. Yet, trying not to deal with your costs will lose your cash over the long haul. You'll most likely wind up paying more expenses than you want to, and it'll play destruction with your monetary determination.

What you can do

By examining and carefully recording receipts for only a couple of moments consistently, you can keep on top of them, stay up with the latest, and save time.

You can utilize a cell phone application or a work area scanner, remembered for some cutting-edge printers.

## 3. Receipt on time

It's not difficult to turn out to be so occupied with normal employment that invoicing gets neglected.

Try not to allow this to occur.If you have any desire to keep cash streaming into your business, you want to receive it when the work is done and acknowledged.

What you can do

On the off chance that a task is especially enormous, you could sort out some way to receive some of it in stages to guarantee you can keep your business running while you work on the undertaking.

Great bookkeeping programming will uphold invoicing, stream information from buy orders, mechanize dreary assignments, and keep away from the tedious and blunder-inclined rekeying of information. Numerous clients will naturally pay inside the concurred period, typically 30 days. Be that as it may, some could require a poke, which carries us to…

4. Ensure your clients pay on time

Nobody likes pursuing clients for installment. All things considered, these are individuals you want to win work from to keep your business developing.You would rather not resent them. Yet, if they've concurred on a charge and a receipt plan, and acknowledged your work, they ought to pay on time. Some could miss installment dates accidentally.BOthers could take a stab at clinging to their money until they truly need to pay.

There might be certain individuals who are in truly monetary difficulty and are frantically shy of money.

What you can do

Search for bookkeeping programming that will follow when solicitations are past due, and either alert you or send a computerized receipt update.

In some cases a robotized update is everything necessary, freeing you from the horrendous undertaking of calling to pursue up your cash.

Furthermore, it's valuable to be in touch with your clients as well.Having an ordinary exchange with them means that assuming they are battling to make an installment on time, you have notification ahead of time and can do whatever it takes to ensure you're not adhered to with regards to payday.

## 5. Computerize your expense

No private company can try not to submit charge reports - and that implies finding and examining heaps of various pieces of data.

Assuming that data is out of control - in paper receipts and solicitations - this turns into an irritating and troublesome errand. You'll presumably put it off till the latest possible second, causing you additional pressure.

Also, assuming you're the sort of individual who neglects to keep receipts, or coincidentally discards them, you can wind up paying more expense than you need to.

What you can do

A significant part of the tax collection cycle can be mechanized by the right programming devices, on the off chance that you stay up with the latest.

On the off chance that you keep records all through the year in your bookkeeping programming, your government form shouldn't for even a moment need to be an agony when the opportunity arrives to document it.

6. Bank continuously

Why trust that a bank proclamation will learn assuming that your funds are battling fit or nearly dead?. Web and versatile finance make it simple to keep steady over your exchanges as they occur - and with the right programming, those exchanges can be consequently accommodated with your business accounts so everything adds up.

What you can do

Most banks offer web-based admittance accounts and a decent bookkeeping programming bundle will consequently pull exchange data from your ledger and accommodate it with your records.

You can be proactive in dealing with your money, spending, speculations, and getting. This will assist your business with getting funds from now on and set it a way to development.

# The Torpid Person's Manual for Acquiring Client

1.Become Findable and Arrangement the Internet Establishments

The initial step is to begin getting people who are now searching for accounting administrations.

Begin by Focusing on Individuals Previously Searching for a Clerk

Individuals search "clerks close to me" on the off chance that they can trust it, and can get in on that activity.

You need to cross with people who are looking for a clerk, need an accounting administration, or use Google to find "accountants for private companies" And that's what other watchwords are like.

The uplifting news is that Google furnishes you with a basic but ultra-successful stage to draw in accounting clients.

Your Google business profile will help you enormously in your interest in crossing with potential accounting clients.

A.   Get a Google business profile arrangement with virtual entertainment: The principal thing you want to do is arrange a Google Business Profile for your accounting business. LISTEN Cautiously and regard my recommendation. Google gives you the neighborhood query items to rank for watchwords that your accounting clients will look at.

Watchwords Accounting clients are looking for:

- Accounting organizations close to me
- Bookkeepers close to me
- Business bookkeepers close to me
- Clerks
- Accounting firms
- Clerks for business
- Business accounting administrations

Essentially every watchword that accounting clients are looking at, drives the nearby guide pack. You Should lay out a Google Business profile for your accounting business, and afterward work to get heaps of surveys.

The main method for getting additional accounting clients is to get your Google business profile arrangement, ensure it's precisely arranged and streamlined, and afterward get Each individual who confides in you or has worked with you, to leave you a survey.

Get surveys from all clients and individuals who trust you.

When you arrange your Google Business, you can just go to research, search your name, and afterward hit the "get more audits" button.

Google will then, at that point, give you a connection that you can text and email to individuals, and they can undoubtedly give a survey.

Individuals needn't bother with being previous clients to ask them for a survey, you could go to previous collaborators, companions, and even family.

The key is to likewise request character reference audits. Get every one individual who trusts you, give you a survey, and you'll be en route to springing up noticeably to each neighborhood entrepreneur searching for a clerk.

The least demanding method for beginning to get surveys is to request character reference audits.

Try not to categorize yourself by disregarding different catch phrases as you do this.

You're not only a clerk, you're known as a bookkeeper as well.

Keep in mind, you're attempting to get accounting clients, however many individuals consider you a bookkeeper, and I feel that clerks owe it to themselves to form a bookkeeping and duty firm that can give a pile of administrations that I call the "re-appropriated bookkeeper model".

While you're developing your Google surveys to rank as an accounting business, you'll need to consider getting your business to rank for watchwords around bookkeeping, duty, CPA, and even finance.

<u>Instructions to Get Audits:</u>

So before I continue toward different plans to get accounting clients, I need to give you some genuine understanding.

- Try not to mess around here about surveys.
- Try not to "Attempt" to get audits, GO GET Surveys.
- Make a rundown of everybody that could give you a survey.
- Call or text that individual
- Send them the connection
- Resend the connection sometime thereafter
- Follow up multiple times
- Be mindful of measuring the value of a survey

Ensure you're a mindful individual while you do this. Uninformed individuals aren't in line with how they're seen, and could wind up requesting surveys from individuals they should not be asking audits for. Try not to be apprehensive, however, know to the point of perceiving that assuming somebody continues to overlook your solicitation for a survey, it very well may be they would truly prefer not to give an audit.

Ask everybody and be persevering, yet additionally be a mindful individual.

You want loads of surveys. I can't stand when individuals think 2-to-5 surveys are sufficient.

Your accounting business will not get additional accounting clients on the off chance that you can't get 20-50 surveys in the long run.

If you battle, you have a more pressing issue - a believability issue.

You want to take care of business and convey results to individuals over the long run to develop your believability on the web, yet it's in every case truly hard while you're beginning without any preparation.

You ought to attempt to get 25-45 Google Surveys

# What number of Audits are Required Before You Get an Accounting Client?

You'll begin drawing in additional accounting clients when you have around 15 or so audits. There's some kind of wizardry in our brain research when individuals notice more than 15 surveys that show you're not some new business (regardless of whether you are)

Your objective ought to be to get more than 15 surveys right away, and afterward, I believe that you should go for that 50-60 audits.

Consider the possibility that I need far-off accounting clients, does this mean I need to meet my bookkeeping client face to face?

By dealing with nearby Website design enhancement and attempting to get neighborhood accounting clients, you don't need to meet anybody face to face. Set the assumption that you're high protein enough that you want to work from a distance and through Zoom or Google Gatherings.

By attempting to rank for neighborhood accounting watchwords with your Google business, you won't need to meet face to face.

What this does, is assist you with exploiting Google's benefit they've given your accounting business. You CAN leap to the front of the line inside a 20-50 mile range around your area if you do things right.

Growing a neighborhood Website optimization presence doesn't mean you can't be remote and work with public clients.

This is only the start of utilizing inbound methodologies to draw in and close accounting clients, yet the beginning is to arrange a business profile for your accounting business and afterward get however many surveys as you can summon.

Imagine a scenario in which You have no clients yet, and You've recently begun your accounting business.

If you're simply beginning and you have no accounting clients to approach, buckle down on getting character reference audits.

B - Arrangement of All Your Center Social Profiles

Other than setting up a Google business profile and getting surveys for your accounting business, you'll likewise need to arrange all your social profiles.

Regardless of whether you mean utilizing web-based entertainment, you want to arrange social profiles and genuine business pages on significant frameworks.

Arrangement each friendly profile and site profile completely, as it prompts better Website optimization

You'll have to ensure that you have reliable naming and naming of your business on this multitude of profiles, and afterward, you will need to guarantee that your contact data is indistinguishable across every one of them.

We want to ensure that you utilize a title reliably across your site, Google My Business, Facebook, LinkedIn, YouTube, TikTok, and Twitter.

Your LLC business name doesn't have to match indistinguishably from the title that you use in your accounting business. Make a title you'll use as your business name, open a DBA assuming that you're truly flabby about promoting a name marginally unique about a name enrolled at the state, and afterward compose that name definitively as the title in your business.

The standard is to have exact and reliable naming, address, telephone number, and titles on every one of your "references" or your profiles on the web.

Do you want a business Facebook page, Instagram page, LinkedIn business page, TikTok business profile, and YouTube business page in 2024?

Indeed, you want to set these up as a result of two reasons:

First, you'll have the option to utilize them to get to a large number of individuals, and

second, they assist with Website optimization for sure.

Social profiles show Google and Bing you exist and you have a heartbeat.

You will need to set up this multitude of web-based entertainment profiles for your business since, supposing that somebody at any point does a marked hunt, the sort of search where they type in your business name into Google, you will need to top off the principal several pages with every one of the profiles that you use.

At the end of the day, we are attempting to tell web indexes that you are a business, that you take care of issues, and we want to stand apart among the trillions of pages across the whole Web.

Setting up business profiles and finishing them up totally on each friendly stage has become one of the center Website optimization beginning stages that will assist your business with hanging out in web search tools, other than providing you with the wide range of various advantages of promoting via virtual entertainment.

One way web crawlers will know your accounting business is dynamic, takes care of business, and isn't spam, is by having social profiles and putting a piece into posting on them.

So indeed, you ought to involve web-based entertainment for your business, and I would open them all.

The primary thing I believe you should know is that you ought to open up a page on every one of the accompanying web-based entertainment stages, and afterward, you ought to submit to certain standards.

It's the underpinning of Computerized showcasing. It's your passageway to a large number of individuals.

What web-based entertainment profiles would it be a good idea for you to open for an Accounting Business?

- Google Business
- YouTube Brand Page
- Facebook business page
- LinkedIn Business page
- Tik tok business page
- Instagram business page
- Apple Guides profile

Once more, ensure that you have a steady naming design, finish them up totally, and afterward put their connections in the footer of your site and on your About page.

The primary thing to do to get accounting clients is to arrange your Google and social profiles and put resources into getting audits.

2 - Make a Site that Sells

You want a business site, and you can't exaggerate web-based entertainment.

Virtual entertainment will sell you out, and except for YouTube, they for the most part lead to less productive and lower-grade organizations.

The truth is that when individuals need to tackle an issue, they ordinarily will take to research to track down an answer.

Google is a door to your site, and you should guarantee that your site works hard by changing guests into clients. Google utilizes your site, YouTube, and your Google business profile to answer inquiries that your potential accounting clients have.

Your site is basic.

Try not to Exaggerate Online Entertainment for Accounting!

Online entertainment can positively be utilized to draw in forthcoming accounting clients and private companies, and you could utilize it to participate in a strong and significant manner to get more clients. An issue with web-based entertainment, especially Instagram, Facebook, and LinkedIn, is that it presently calls for enormous time ventures and content creation to appear before individuals, and afterward, they're for the most part in a thoughtless state contrasted with an answer disapproved of mentality

The issue with virtual entertainment is that individuals are not pondering arrangements while they are utilizing it, they are carelessly looking over.

Starting around 2024, virtual entertainment additionally remunerates things like reels and shorts, which certainly stand out and will generally prompt much less business results.

The stuff to appear in an online entertainment feed is frequently contradictory to the stuff to have someone make a stride with your business.

To put it plainly, I suggest that you are cautious about concentrating profoundly via virtual entertainment contrasted with your site, Google business profile, and YouTube channel.

What are the most significant pages for your business? Your site, YouTube channel, and Google business profile.

We should simply say there's a motivation behind why Facebook, LinkedIn, and Instagram are confronting gigantic decays.

Try not to exaggerate virtual entertainment posting, since natural reach isn't probably going to happen effectively so incline toward paid.

Motivations behind why you shouldn't exaggerate virtual entertainment for business:

You could challenge me on that and think that web-based entertainment is totally where you will get great clients, and I'm not saying you're off-base. You can surely use Instagram, TickTock, and LinkedIn to get clients, however, I find that the RRY can be tested except if you stick to making astounding substances.

Eating useful content, positions you as an aide, and is then shared across all stages is the center to prevailing via virtual entertainment.

The following are several reasons that I figure virtual entertainment action for your business ought to be controlled and you shouldn't invest a lot of energy presenting and taking a stab at getting "reach".

3 Motivations Not to Exaggerate Online Entertainment Showcasing for Bookkeepers:
- It double-crosses you
- They need to track you down in search.

- You can drive monstrous traffic with advertisements

1 - It Sells out You:

Most importantly, web-based entertainment monsters famously mess around with their calculations and they reward the absolute lowest grade patterns and exercises. The stage won't compensate you because as a rule, attempting to take care of individual broccoli and help them to do what they want. Individuals are for the most part in a careless state via virtual entertainment, or they could engage in their interests and interests, however, they're not commonly prepared to make a ton of moves and online entertainment has an extraordinarily short life expectancy.

The motivation behind why virtual entertainment double-crosses you is that each post you make has an extremely short life expectancy and they mess around with their calculations so it takes serious commitment to request to persistently appear in people groups.

You'll likewise see that virtual entertainment has chosen to mess around in political decision cycles and control of reach. At the impulses of a mediator or a reality checker, your whole profile can get closed down if you say some unacceptable thing regarding any gathering.

At the point when you use Facebook, Instagram, TickTock, or LinkedIn, you are obliged to their directives and you don't have a lot of opportunities.

## 2 - Search is generally significant

Second, social posts on Facebook, Instagram, and TikTok don't do quite a bit of anything to assist you with appearing in Google, Alexa, or Bing Searches when individuals are hoping to Take care of Issues.

## 3 - You can simply utilize advertisements

Last, you ought to realize that web-based entertainment for business is truly an arrangement to make you burn through cash on promotions.

You can without much of a stretch get the majority of the advantages of these stages by basically running some publicizing.

I bring it all up because I see an excessive number of clerks focus profoundly on making very imaginative diagrams, virtual entertainment designs, and web-based entertainment presents just to have them vanish and never benefit them after about 14 days. Your virtual entertainment has an unbelievably short life expectancy and shelf life, and I would possibly present sufficient show-up when individuals are checking your profile out. I see that as it's generally critical to guarantee that individuals see a decent arrangement of expert and supportive posts on your page when they coincidentally find it while exploring during their "edification deals stage" when they approve that you're a decent arrangement.

Virtual entertainment can be a significant asset hoard and lead to next to no business if you don't watch out.

Your Site then again, is strategic.

Your site, YouTube channel, and Google business profile are the main promoting devices you'll at any point have if you use them appropriately.

What does it take to make a site that positions and sells for your accounting business?

3 - Make a video direct mail advertising and video content

Another tip we have while beginning an accounting business or virtual accounting business, is to make a video direct mail advertisement.

Selling is difficult work, and a video can do it for you in your rest.

A Video Direct mail advertisement is a video you'll put on your site that will situate yourself to likely clients, as opposed to expecting individuals to peruse your site and publicize duplicates.

The third thing you ought to do is make a 45 - 240 second video direct mail advertisement, that quickly conveys all the informing and situating we referenced in your site content.

Individuals like to simply hit play and not need to peruse, and a video can truly assist you with changing over that data quickly.

Other than having the option to briefly change over what you offer, the issue you tackle, and how you improve their life, individuals can get to realize you a tad,

Individuals purchase from individuals, and the more you let people figure out your character, and assist them with seeing you as an extraordinary answer to their concerns, the more probable they will be to change over with you.

Put resources into a decent video direct mail advertisement.

Here are a few hints:

- Begin by rapidly referencing what your identity is, and the center administrations you offer.

Here are the straightforward pieces of a decent video direct mail advertisement.

What your identity is

What you do

Who you serve

The center issue you tackle

Significant ways you work on their life

How they need to make a stride

- Begin by rapidly snaring the audience to tell them they're perfectly located, that you give an answer and it's to them.

- Individuals don't tune in until they realize something is for them, and afterward, they truly don't tune in until they understand what's going on with it and how it will help them.

I in every case rapidly finish and bounce directly into their concern.

Video Direct mail advertisement Parts Recap:

- What your identity is
- What you do
- Who you serve
- The center issue you tackle
- Significant ways you work on their life
- How they need to make a stride

Video direct mail advertisements replace a cold pitch - you can send it to individuals through cool messages, and it will help you in countless ways.

- Use on your site - Everybody will have a potential chance to get to know you and hear how you make them flourish.

- Use in cool messages and messages - You can undoubtedly utilize this, alongside your CRM, to associate with individuals.

- Use in online entertainment informing - These recordings can be made into virtual entertainment posts and promoting that truly cover the center features of how you help individuals.

- Use Youtube Guard Promotions - You can utilize YouTube to do a few astonishing things.

To get additional accounting clients, you'll need to make a video like I recently depicted.

The most effective method to Record and Film Your Video Direct mail advertisement:

7 Speedy Tips on Really Recording a Video Direct Mail Advertisement:

- Get spotless sound.
- Utilize a proficient videographer OR your iPhone in a peaceful room
- Compose the content and practice it 10-15 times.
- At the point when you convey it, don't hold excessively close to the content
- Grin and Immediately Convey
- Don't overcomplicate it
- Talk quickly - don't burn through individuals' time.

4 - Prospect and Warm Call

Okay, assuming you go to help like Deals Genie, you can get a rundown of organizations' drives that you can then expertly approach.

If you need a genuine business, you want to prospect.

The best clients view you from video, search, or in-person calls/organizing/references.

On the off chance that you need a genuine business that has high retainer clients, you'll have to prospect.

I prescribe that you essentially acquaint yourself with 10 individuals every day, 3 days per week, on Tuesday, Wednesday, and Thursday.

Doing so will get you before 1500 individuals, and furnish you with leads.

If 8% will make a stride with you, and a fourth of those become a client, you'll get around 30 clients from that.

Front-end action and VOLUME of clients will prompt great customers, "noticeably flawed showcasing".

On the off chance that you call each worker for hire in your space and say "Hello, I'm … … and I own an accounting business not too far off, I was contemplating whether I could shoot you an email so you have my data assuming that you at any point need an accounting organization", you'll come by great outcomes.

Truly, high-protein organizations are utilized as proficient agents.

You can utilize Deals Genie to get Business contacts, and afterward use Hubspot to connect with them and monitor things.

5 - Develop Authority and Believability
This is gigantic, you want to Make CONTENT on your site and YouTube channel.
If you answer questions, educate, and cover topics in a very careful way, you will end up being a greatly fruitful clerk.

You can make guides on Quickbooks, you can tell the best way to import information from project worker programming, and you can show the best way to decrease charges as an XYZ or no difference either way.

The key is you want to make content on your foundation so that individuals see you're a power.

Other than that, you want to get client surveys, video tributes, and hotshot all the great road validity you're getting.

Request that your clients send you recordings saying you've assisted them with remaining coordinated.

Ask them for a statement, utilize a structure on your site, and ask them for a tweet-capable statement.

Last, you want those Google audits and as you do this, you'll get ready to be overwhelmed with Search engine optimization and individuals that see your substance will not have the option to remain away.

6 - Several Advertisements with Remarketing

Paid search promotions are truly strong for accounting organizations.

You want to remain before individuals who have been to your site.

One of our administrations here at Feedback Wrench is to assist you with conveying basic paid search promoting, lead magnet advertisements, video direct mail advertisement publicizing, and remarketing efforts.

What's more, we suggest beginning with a paid inquiry add around catchphrases like "clerks close to me, accounting administrations, accounting organizations, bookkeepers close to me, bookkeeping organizations, business bookkeepers, charge prep close to me, business charges close to me, CPA close to me and so forth."

Then, at that point, you can utilize a lead magnet in remarketing to them.

Paid Search promotions, combined with retargeting are the best key publicizing.

A comment is the point at which you present a promotion on Facebook, YouTube, Google Show, and different stages to individuals who've previously seen your items on YouTube, been to your site, tapped on a promotion, or generally connected with you here and there, shape or structure.

I, as a rule, suggest running paid search promotions that likewise have an area expansion showing their Google surveys.

I likewise prescribe zeroing in on a 30 to 50-mile circle around your center help region so your Google surveys will show in the ad.

Quick version, these promotions will work and the remarketing keeps your name before them so they will truly need to work with you after some time.

# Chapter 3:Step -by-step instructions to make Accounting simple

There are 7 moves toward making your accounting simple

Separate your own and operational expense

Make your entrance

Pick a bookkeeping technique: accumulation or money

Get the right apparatuses

Arrange your exchanges

Take on a framework for putting away your reports

Track down your allowances

Stage 1: Separate Your Own and Costs of Doing Business

The absolute first thing you'll believe should do is open a business financial balance so you can isolate your costs from your operational expense.

The explanation for this is so significant that it reduces to responsibility. Assuming that you're running an LLC or a partnership and your operational expenses are completely turned inside out, it's conceivable that you could be expected to take responsibility for any obligations obtained by the organization.

Blending the two can likewise bring about incredible cerebral pain when it comes time to record charges. Besides the fact that it results in a missed derivation, however, it will probably make your CPA invest more energy doing your expenses. The two situations will cost you cash.

Stage 2: Make Your Entrance
The following thing you'll have to do is conclude which accounting method you will utilize: single-passage or twofold section.

Single-passage implies that every exchange is recorded once, either as pay or as a cost. Resources and liabilities (like gear, stock, and credits) are independently followed. On the off chance that you're in the earliest reference point phases of beginning your organization or are still in the leisure activity stage, a single section will suit you fine and dandy. It's fast, simple, and satisfactory for fundamental-level accounting.

The twofold section is more modern, yet additionally more exact and smart. It is more qualified for laid-out organizations that are past the leisure activity stage.

With twofold section accounting, all exchanges are kept in a diary, then everything is placed into the overall record twice — as a charge and a credit.

Practically all bookkeeping programming depends on twofold section accounting as it is the strategy utilized by proficient clerks and bookkeepers.

Stage 3: Pick A Bookkeeping Technique: Accumulation or Money
You'll likewise have to conclude which bookkeeping technique you will utilize. Your choices are restricted to gathering or money.

With cash bookkeeping, exchanges are recorded whenever cash has been traded. If you charge a client today, that cash isn't kept in that frame of mind until the installment is gotten.

A lot of independent ventures utilize the money technique since it's basic and direct; you don't need to follow receivables and payables, in addition, you'll know precisely the amount of money you possess close-by out of the blue.

With gathering bookkeeping, pay is recorded when the client is charged (regardless of whether installment isn't expected for one more month) as records receivable. A similar rule applies for costs; the exchange is recorded when you're charged as records payable.

Gathering bookkeeping is typically better for greater, more settled organizations. It provides you with a drawn-out perspective on your business' pay and costs that money bookkeeping can't give.

Stage 4: Order Your Exchanges

Each exchange that happens should be appropriately ordered when it's placed into your books. This assists you with finding more duty derivations and will make your life a ton simpler. Would it be a good idea for you to get examined (hope for the best)?

Suppose, for instance, that a half year down the line you run over a plain supper receipt. Was this from a gathering with a planned client? Or on the other hand was it an organization outing? Sorting these exchanges as they happen will save you from accomplishing analytical work later on.

Stage 5: Get The Right Devices

In the former times, each exchange must be physically placed using pencil and paper. It was a careful interaction without a doubt. Luckily, that is not true anymore because the present day progresses in innovation.

Presently, there are bookkeeping programming programs that make dealing with your books quicker and more straightforward — yet some are superior to other people.

## Stage 6: Embrace a Framework for Putting away Your Records

At the point when you document your duties, you must demonstrate the legitimacy of your costs. That is the reason keeping monetary records is so significant.

Similarly significant is ensuring that these records are put away in a safe area. Since the IRS acknowledges computerized records, we suggest utilizing a cloud-based framework like Dropbox, Google Drive, or Evernote. In addition to the fact that it saves you actual space, however, you'll likewise have the option to get to these records from any area.

## Stage 7: Track down Your Allowances

A derivation, by and large, should meet the accompanying rules: a) it is a conventional cost in your industry and b) it is essential.

So, regardless of whether a cost is both customary and important, that doesn't mean you can deduct the full expense on your assessments. Assuming you telecommute two times every week

## The straightforward accounting strategy (for individuals who can't stand intricacy)

Single-section accounting

Single-section accounting is a direct technique where one passage is made for every exchange in your books. These exchanges are typically kept up within a money book to follow approaching income and active costs. You don't require formal bookkeeping to prepare for the single-section framework. The single-section technique will suit little privately owned businesses and sole ownerships that don't trade using a loan, own practically zero actual resources, and hold modest quantities of stock.

This strategy for accounting is a straightforward record of pay and costs utilizing a manual money book and number cruncher, or a bookkeeping sheet in a self-computing system like Open Office, Microsoft Succeed, or Quattro Genius.

The Cash Book Sections Made sense of

The Date - This is the date of the exchange which you can get off the bookkeeping source records.

Portrayal - A short depiction of the exchange. You can put anything that data you feel is vital, however, don't go overboard!

Reference - You can fundamentally pick anything reference will assist you with recognizing the exchange. Certain individuals utilize the receipt numbers or the initials of the kind of installment exchange (like DC for Direct Credit). The reference can be composed in some place on the exchange report if it's not on there as of now - like a receipt number. This is a decent method of cross-referring to the exchange and installment between the cashbook and the record.

Pay/Costs - Just supplement the worth of the exchange into the fitting section... is it cash coming into the business or cash leaving the business? You could change the headings to 'Cash In' and 'Cash Out' on the off chance that you prefer. Bank - This is a running equilibrium segment that changes each time an exchange is placed. Add the pay, and take away the costs. Notice on 01 Apr there is an initial equilibrium. This is the equilibrium taken from the last day in Spring and presented (b/f) to Apr. It can likewise be called b/d - cut down.

You can figure out more about the cashbook organization and plan your one assuming that you like it to suit your necessities.

All exchanges will fall under five record types: income, costs, value, resources, and liabilities. Individual sections are then coordinated into subcategories called accounts. If you run a pizza parlor, for instance, a few records in your record could peruse "income pizza deals," or "costs pizza fixings."

So, how you order exchanges will rely upon your industry and business, which is the reason we suggest talking with an expert when you set up your books.